THE LORD'S PRAYER

Our Father which art in heaven, Hallowed be thy name. thy kingdom come. Thy will be done in earth, as it is in heaven. Give us this day our daily bread. And forgive us our debts, as we forgive our debtors. And lead us not into temptation, but deliver us from evil: For thine is the kingdom, and the power, and the glory, for ever. Amen.

Matt. 6: 9-13

Christ's Mould Of Prayer

By
James Allan Francis, D.D.

Copyright 1924
By
James Allan Francis
Reprint Edition by Dauphin Publications, 2022
ISBN 978-1-939438-77-5

Christ's Mould of Prayer

WHEN we turn to a very familiar passage in the Bible, we are always in danger of thinking that, because we know it by heart, we really know it. May I ask you, for a little while, to rethink one of the most familiar passages in the whole Book and, as far as such a thing is possible, to think of it freshly as if you had never heard or seen it before. I refer to the passage commonly known as "The Lord's Prayer."

The gospel according to Luke 5 tells us that Jesus was praying. The disciples were listening. Can you imagine that experience? It is easy to believe that it seemed to them as if they had never heard anybody really

3

PRAY before. Such tenderness, such boldness, such sympathy, such self-forgetfulness, such humility, such largeness of petition, such nearness to God, such agony of passion, such supreme energy! They were indeed overhearing the very secrets of heaven. I wonder if there is not a significance in the fact that, while Jesus prayed often for his disciples and while he taught them how to pray, there is no record that he ever prayed with his disciples. We have no account of his ever saying: "Let us pray." There seems to have been an aloneness, a separateness, not only from sinners, but from saints as well, in the prayer life of our Lord.

On this occasion, when he ceased, as soon as they dared to break the silence, one of them, doubtless voicing the desire of all, said: "Lord, teach us to pray, as John also taught his disciples." No request ever pleased Jesus more than this. He began at

4

once to answer it, and the first great lesson on prayer was a pattern of prayer. We do not for a moment suppose that the Master intended we should always use these words and these only. Indeed, even Matthew and Luke differ in their accounts. Nevertheless, these words, brief as they are, give us a complete outline map of the whole continent of prayer. I question if any Christian has breathed a true prayer in nineteen centuries that did not logically fall under the head of one of these petitions. It is the most comprehensive piece of literature in the language of earth and "the most precious religious document in the possession of the human race." When Jesus framed these words, he probably made the largest single contribution to the religious knowledge of mankind ever made at one time. The prayer is so simple that it fits the lips and heart of childhood; yet it is so profound that the greatest intellectual giant has not fathomed its depths. I wonder if he ever did anything that marked him off more clearly as the divine Son of God and the Master Thinker of the ages than did the creation of this single paragraph. It contains, in the King James translation of the Matthew version, only sixty-five words; it can be read without hurrying in two minutes; but in it Jesus bares the heart of man like an open book, and at the same time bares the heart of God, and then brings the two together. When they meet they fit as the ocean fits the shore. One can see at a glance that there never can be a need either in the individual or in the collective life of the race, but that there is a corresponding fullness in God to meet that need so perfectly that we "are complete in him." Please notice how all sides of the relationship between God and the soul are here expressed.

"Our Father which art in heaven"; here is a child addressing his father. "Hallowed be thy name"; here is a worshiper addressing his God. "Thy kingdom come"; here is a citizen approaching his king. "Thy will be done on earth as it is in heaven"; here is a servant speaking to his master. "Give us this day our daily bread"; a beggar to his benefactor. "Forgive us our debts, as we forgive our debtors"; a sinner to his Saviour. "Lead us not into temptation"; a pilgrim to his guide. "But deliver us from evil"; a captive to his deliverer. What then is God to me? A Father, a God, a King, a Master, a Benefactor, a Saviour, a Guide and a Deliverer. And what am I to him? A child, a worshiper, a citizen, a servant, a beggar, a sinner, a pilgrim and a captive seeking deliverance. And all this in sixty-five words. A man's mind, unaided, could no more have struck off this prayer than a man's hand could have scooped up the Pacific Ocean, ridged up the Rocky Mountains, or hung the sun upon the brow of yonder sky. Imagine this task presented to one of you. Take God's plan for the ages, world-wide and eternity-long, put into it all that he ever intends to do in the life of mankind in this world and the next. Add to this all the deep and varied needs of the human heart, individual and collective. Then add the story of the divine fullness to meet these needs; sum it all up and express it in six phrases that can be read in two minutes. You answer, *Impossible*. Human speech will break under the strain; human effort cannot compass such a task. Well, that is exactly what Jesus Christ has done for us in this prayer. It is not mere accident that his words have lived. They have in them the thoughts of God distilled in human speech, and they will live on when suns have burned out and stars have fallen like autumn leaves.

Let us examine the prayer a little, clause by clause. "When ye pray, say Our Father"— better pause here. These two

8

words, "Our Father," are the golden hinges on which the door of this treasure house swings open. If your heart enters into the meaning of these two words, you may go on with the rest of this prayer. If not, it will hardly be worth while, for the rest of the prayer depends for its value and power to you on the meaning you find in these two words, "Our Father." This is the greatest thing Christ ever told mankind about God. Not only so, but he repeated this message oftener than any other. It was his favorite formula. Remember his first public word preserved for us, spoken in the Temple when he was a lad of only twelve: "Wist ye not that I must be about my *Father's* business?" Remember his last word on the cross: "Father, into thy hands I commend my spirit." Remember the first word, when he rose from the dead: "Go to my brethren, and say unto them, I ascend unto my Father, and your Father." Again, remember his last words, before he disappeared through the clouds into heaven: "Behold, I send the promise of my Father upon you." Christ's supreme message to men was, "God is your Father." With it, of course, goes the corollary, "Mankind are the children of God." Indeed, it is not too much to say that the whole revelation of Christ, his lowly birth, his holy life, his miracles of power, his deeds of mercy, his matchless sermons, his redeeming death, his triumphant resurrection, his glorious ascension and the gift of the Spirit through his mighty intercession – is simply God's own interpretation of his fatherhood toward men. It is the fatherhood of God interpreted in the redeeming love of the Son. When you go into the secret place and shut the door and say "Father," you are face to face with the last ultimate reality in the nature of God. When you say "Our Father," you express the entire socialism of the Kingdom of Heaven.

The six petitions that follow fall naturally into two groups of three each. As we read the first three, we note that the clause added to the third petition, "in earth, as it is in heaven," does not belong exclusively to it, but equally to each of the three. To get its full meaning, you would read it thus: "Hallowed be thy name in earth as it is in heaven. Thy kingdom come in earth as it is in heaven." How much did the Master teach us to ask for when he told us to use these words? How much change must there be in this world of ours before this prayer will be answered to his satisfaction? Is there a day coming when every human heart will love God; when everyone will love others with a love like that wherewith Christ loves us; when every business transaction on earth will be conducted by the principles and in the spirit of the Sermon on the Mount; when every relationship between husband and wife, parent and child, teacher and student, employer and employee, friend and friend, ruler and ruled, will be according to the very heart of Christ; when in all the literature of the world, there will not be a book that Jesus would be ashamed to have written; when in all the art galleries there will not be a picture that he would be ashamed to have painted; when every realm of human thought and activity, everything that touches the life of mankind on this earth, shall be so permeated, controlled, energized, uplifted, transfigured and glorified by the indwelling spirit of Christ, that the life of man on this earth will reflect the life of God as the unruffled lake reflects the sun? When that day comes, this prayer will have been answered – then and not till then.

When they said "teach us to pray," instead of giving them some little kindergarten lessons, drawn from their immediate needs or surroundings, he lifted his eyes and swept the far horizon of God; he gathered up the ultimate dream of the eternal; he rounded the sum of things, all God ever intends to do in the life of mankind; and then, packing it all in these three terse pregnant phrases, he said: "After this manner therefore pray ye." Nor was this the dream of some hour of singular ecstasy. The significant fact is that, in the darkest hour of his life, when everything seemed to go against him, he never fell below this level. A scepter universal, undisputed, undivided, was his constant anticipation. His ultimate kingdom will be no whit smaller than the line fence that he staked out at the beginning. He was giving his own horizon to his disciples. He was speaking to the twentieth century – to the fortieth if need be – as well as to the first.

What an amazing contrast between this and much of the praying that I have done. When I follow the lead of my own heart, I pray thus: "Oh, Lord, bless ME"; then, *my* family, *my* church, *my* city, *my* country," and away on the far fringe as I end, there may be a prayer for the extension of his kingdom throughout the wide parish of the world. The Master begins where I left off. He puts the world first and my personal needs second. Only after my prayer has crossed every continent and touched every far-flung island of the sea, only after it has taken in the last man in the last backward race, only after it has covered the entire wish and purpose of God for the world, only then am I taught to ask for a piece of bread for myself. Is the great commission itself more distinctly missionary than this? Evidently, then, the supreme use of prayer is not to get things for myself but to forward God's kingdom on earth. This prayer contemplated a man so wrapped up in, and enamored of, the great program of Christ that it fills all the foreground of his thinking and feeling. Only after he has poured out his soul for that which is the master passion of his being, does he ask for the supply of his own needs; and this, only in order that he may be equipped and sustained to do Christ's work. Is this too much to ask? Is the standard too high? When the young man gives himself in love to the one who is his heart's choice, what does he ask in return? Only that she shall do the same. When the Lord Jesus gives himself to us, gives us all in the holy extravagance of the cross, is it too much if he asks us to do the same? Hear the tentmaker of Tarsus, as he writes from a Roman prison: "I would ye should understand, brethren, that the things which have happened unto me...." What things? Why, this imprisonment and all that goes with it of hardship and privation. "The things which have happened unto me have fallen out rather unto the furtherance of the gospel." You can hear that shout of consecrated triumph across nineteen wide centuries. Here is a man to whom home, friends, comfort, freedom, even life itself, dear as they are, are of secondary importance beside the one consuming purpose that Christ's business should be pushed and his name known to the farthest bounds of the habitable globe. It was such character as this that Jesus Christ aimed to build when he gave them this prayer. No man or woman ever amounts to much in the kingdom, no one touches even the edge of God's zone of power until this lesson is learned and heartily accepted: that Christ's business is the supreme concern in this world and that all personal matters, however dear or important, are tributary thereto.

Robert Moffatt, the veteran African missionary and explorer, after a third of a century of service, was visiting a home in old England. He was asked to write something original in a young lady's album. He wrote this:

"My album is a savage breast,
Where tempests brood and shadows rest
Without one ray of light.
To write the name of Jesus there,
And point to the worlds more bright and fair,
And see that savage bow in prayer,
This is my soul's delight."

When we turn now to the second half of the prayer, we are struck with the contrast between the vast sweep of the first three petitions and the exceeding modesty of the second three. There is a beautiful translation in an old Moravian version of Scriptures of the saying of Gabriel to Mary concerning her son. It reads in our King James version, "And of his kingdom there shall be no end." The Moravians render it, "And his kingdom shall have no frontier." There was a time when our western frontier in America was at the Allegheny Mountains. Then it moved on to the Mississippi, then to the Rockies, then to the Pacific, then to the Hawaiian Islands, and finally to the Philippines; this places our western frontier away around in the east. But what is this about Christ's kingdom? "His kingdom shall have no frontier." There is to be no place in the universe, material or spiritual, where a man may stand and say, "The kingdom of Christ stops here."

Note now in contrast the measure of the three that follow. Master! After I have prayed for the carrying out of thy purpose through the length and breadth of the world, what may I ask for my own self? Just three things. Daily bread, daily forgiveness and daily leading. (Feed me, forgive me and keep me straight.) Even these three things I have no right to ask for unless I am living for the three things in the first half of the prayer. I cannot expect God to pay my board another day unless I am living for the hallowing of his name, the coming of his kingdom, and the doing of his will. He may do it, for "he is kind unto the unthankful and to the evil," but have no claim for daily blessings unless I am in the line of daily service.

It was a stormy night in winter when two men came hurrying into a little station on the Highland Railway to catch the train for Edinburgh. Both men were just in time to see the rear lights of the last car as it pulled out of the station. One of them was a nearby farmer. Turning to the station agent, he said, "Last train tonight, sir?" "Last train tonight," was the curt reply. With a half audible expression of disgust, he turned up his coat collar, plunged into the storm and trudged off home. He was only going down to the city on some private business of his own; no one was seriously inconvenienced but himself. The other man, however, was a peer of the realm. He was a member of His Majesty's Privy Council. "Did I understand you, sir, that that was the last train tonight?" "Last train tonight, my Lord." "Have me a special from Aberdeen at once, please. I want to catch the morning express at Edinburgh in order to be in London tomorrow evening in time for an important meeting of the Council." The station master jumped to the ticker, and in fifteen minutes there was a special on its way from Aberdeen to pick up one man at a wayside station so that he could catch his train for London, and the British Empire paid the bill. Why? The best of reasons why. His errand to London was not his own business at all, but the business of the Empire. Hence the resources of the Empire were at his command. God gives no promises to a selfish, self-centered life. If your plans begin and end with yourself, it looks as if you would have to get along the best way you can. But if you are making your supreme end the hallowing of his great name, the coming of his everlasting kingdom and the doing of his holy will, he *could* charter a million suns out of yonder sky and hitch every one of them to your little chariot. Talk about "getting into the swim" –this is the swim, this is the way to launch your tiny craft on the current of God's Niagara and to have behind you the resistless might of the Eternal.

The first half of this prayer is God's program. The second half is God's supply for our personal needs while we help carry out the program.

But do we not meet a dreadful anti-climax in the fourth petition? Think of coming down from the vision of a world-wide spiritual kingdom that shall stand forever to a piece of bread for your dinner. The more we think of it the more strange it seems. How big are we anyway? There are about sixteen hundred millions of people on our earth, and we are just individuals. Our earth itself is but a pin point in the empire of God. Lord Kelvin told us a while ago that the time would probably come when astronomers would take cognizance of the existence of a thousand million suns and worlds, and that this world of ours is one of the very smallest in the whole great family. If God were to send an angel out from heaven to look for our world with no celestial chart to guide him, it would be like sending a little boy out on a Kansas prairie to find a particular blade of grass. And we are but individuals–one out of sixteen hundred millions–crawling around on this little speck of star dust. Are we really to believe that an infinite God, who is the source, support and end of this vast and seemingly limitless system, will come down and trouble himself about our daily bread?

But stay, we are forgetting one important item. Man is a spirit. This alters everything. It matters nothing that the mountains are bigger and the ocean stronger. Man's place in creation does not depend on his physical size at all. We can think God's thoughts after him. We can co-operate with him. Each of us can be a "friend of God." This is more than can be said of all the systems of all the stars. The moment we begin to look at the human soul from God's point of view, we see that there is no anti-climax here whatever. When the Lord Jesus said that one human soul outweighed the world in value, he was not using a figure of speech, but stating a fact. There are more creative wonders in the soul of the humblest human being than in the whole realm of nature, and measured by his possibilities for the future, each human soul is greater than the world on which it lives. What awful honor Christ puts upon us when, after teaching us to soar on the wings of God's plan and to pray for the fulfillment of his vast enterprise, he encourages us to follow with "give us this day our daily bread."

"Forgive us our debts." This clause occasions no surprise. The normal honest man would have wondered if it had been omitted. He is a strange man, who can approach God in prayer without being distinctly conscious of the limitation and embarrassments caused by his own sin. Granted a holy and loving God, the prayer for forgiveness rises naturally to our lips. It is the conclusion of this sentence that sentence that gives us pause: "As we forgive our debtors." Then, these two things, God's forgiveness of us and our forgiveness of our brothers, hath God joined together so that none can put them asunder. It takes the same temper to receive forgiveness as to show forgiveness. If we can do one we can do the other. Indeed, it is the divine forgiveness

24

that shows us how to forgive, and it is the exercise of this grace to a fellow that enables us to understand God's mercy to us.

"Lead us not into temptation, but deliver us from evil." Temptation is the common lot of man. We must not pray to be saved from being tempted, for that is a prayer the Lord does not answer. Indeed, temptation is part of the spiritual machinery of the universe for the making of character. And the very essence of temptation is that it is unexpected. We have not passed this way before. How shall we keep from trembling at the shadow of tomorrow? Our Father will be the same tomorrow that he is today. We must take his offered hand and boldly say, "Lead us not into temptation, but deliver us from evil." We will be bound up in the bundle of life with One who is stronger than any temptation and who will lend his strength to us.

When our hearts are so melted by the Spirit's gracious power that we pray this prayer with fullness of meaning, we are allowing ourselves to be poured into his mould and will come out bearing more distinctly his image.

www.ingramcontent.com/pod-product-compliance
Lightning Source LLC
Chambersburg PA
CBHW010304040426
42331CB00038BA/3356